F. S. A Bourne

The Lo-Fou Mountains

An excursion

F. S. A Bourne

The Lo-Fou Mountains
An excursion

ISBN/EAN: 9783337289003

Printed in Europe, USA, Canada, Australia, Japan

Cover: Foto ©Andreas Hilbeck / pixelio.de

More available books at **www.hansebooks.com**

THE
LO-FOU MOUNTAINS

An Excursion

BY

F. S. A. BOURNE

H. B. M. VICE CONSUL

CANTON

HONGKONG

PRINTED BY KELLY & WALSH, LIMITED

AND AT

SHANGHAI, SINGAPORE & YOKOHAMA

1895

CONTENTS.

I. CANTON TO THE TOP...   1

II. PUT-WAN TZE TO SU-LIU KUN... ...   18

III. SU-LIU KUN BY WAY OF CH'UNG-HÜ
KUN TO CANTON...   31

IV. SECOND TRIP—BY WAY OF TSANG-
SHING   38

APPENDIX A.—Itinerary and Map   42

   „   B.—Altitudes   43

   „   C.—Latitudes and Longitudes   44

   „   D.—Plants collected   45

THE LO-FOU MOUNTAINS.

I.—CANTON TO THE TOP.

In 1892, late in August, when heat and dulness have brought European life in Canton to an irreducible ebb, and when the White Man can only curse the fate that transplanted him in a site so hot and crowded as the delta of the Canton River, a restless Irishman was wandering about an office in Shamien, jerking out: "too many sherries last night, my friend; " feel as if I were a compound of ice-cream, " paté and alcohol; we *must* get away from " this place; ever heard of the Lo-fou Moun- " tains; 4,000 feet high, they say, monastery " on the top, tigers, monkeys; let's go there " and get out of the heat."

This happy inspiration led five Britons to make the excursion of which this paper is an account.

The Lo-fou Mountains lie about 60 miles East of Canton and 70 miles as the crow flies North of Hongkong on the confines of three Districts (縣), the South-Eastern part of the range belonging to Pok-lo* (博羅), the Northern part to Tsang shing (增城) and the South-Western to part Tung-kun (東莞).

---

* Names of places are transliterated from the local (Cantonese) pronunciation.

At 10 a.m. on the 17th September 1892, our launch towing a small house-boat left the Bund; we steamed past Whampoa and turned into the East River at 1.30 p.m. The afternoon was very hot—indeed on our return we found that we had passed on the roof of a small launch, protected only by a thin awning, the hottest day of 1892, the maximum temp. of which is given in the Hongkong Returns as 94° Fahr. Before we had been long in the East River we could make out the Lo-fou range to the North. At dusk we ran aground about a mile below Shek-lung (石龍), and it was not till midnight that we were safely anchored off that very dirty and bad-smelling town.

Here we had to turn our backs on the River, and trust ourselves to Chinese roads and our baggage to porters. We had hoped to be off at daylight the next morning; but nothing could be more dismal than our outlook when at last the light broke. The mountains were hidden in mist; all that we could see from our boat was the squalid straggling suburb; there was no sign of the coolies who were to carry our baggage a long day's journey; and at 6 a.m. it was raining and appeared likely to rain all day.

As twenty miles of unknown road stretched between us and our proposed sleeping place, we did not spare our native staff either remonstrances or threats; and after we had

landed some of them in the rain, which seemed
to raise them to a just sense of the occasion,
the porters came straggling up one by one.
Having got through as well as we could the
inevitable shouting, bullying, objections to the
weight and to the division of the loads, &c.,
incidental to getting coolies to start on a land
journey in China, at about 7.30 a.m. we
marched off, skirting the right or North bank
of the river, up stream. In less than a mile
we turned our backs on the river and went
North straight for the mountains.

Before further describing the journey it
may be useful to future tourists in these parts
to give some account of our equipage. For
this stage from Shek-lung to the foot of the
mountains two of us took sedan-chairs, which
were used occasionally : the other three walked
the whole way. Our baggage, including camp-
beds, cooking vessels, &c., was carried by ten
coolies, being packed as far as possible into
the regular baskets, one of which makes one
side of a coolie's load. We paid the chair and
baggage coolies one dollar each for this day.
Afterwards we engaged coolies from stage
to stage paying them about 50 cents a day
each.

By the time we were well on our way, it
had settled down to a heavy rain. We were
crossing a rice plain often on narrow mud
paths and in a high wind, and our progress
was therefore slow. At about 10.30 a.m. we

reached Ti-ch'ong (鐵塲) about seven miles from Shek-lung, where we had lunch.

At 11.30 a.m. we left Ti-ch'ong going North in such heavy rain that we could see nothing. At 2 p.m. we were winding among the low hills that form the outliers of the range. At 3 p.m. we passed a temple named Fa-shau Tze (花手寺), Temple of the Flower Hand, at the foot of the mountains, which we shall mention again. The climb now began, and at 4 p.m. we reached a large Buddhist Monastery—Wa-shau Toi (華首臺), Terrace of Variegated Heads, 580 feet above the sea, our destination, after a walk from Shek-lung of not less than 21 miles.

A broad winding road leads up to the Monastery through over-hanging woods, the ground covered with a rich under-growth of flowering shrubs, creepers and tall grasses. We pass a stone on which the characters Lo-fou (羅浮) are deeply engraved—said to be the oldest inscription in these mountains; and here and there the rocks are cut with the name of Amida Buddha. Then we heard the low mellow tones of the temple bell—its deep cadence, striking the ear in the solitude of the woods and streams, seemed to carry a sense of awe and repose to the mind, and to turn one's thoughts to something deeper than man's affairs. The Monastery is delightfully situated on a broad terrace to which a stream of clear water descends by a waterfall. The terrace is backed

on the North by the main mass of the mountain breaking away on the East and West into
craggy declivities covered with grand old
trees. Our path approaches from the South.
The buildings are spacious and solid with com-
fortable guest rooms, and quarters for one or
two hundred monks. There is a lavatory—a
rare sight in China—and a very curious one.
The mountain stream is diverted by a small
aqueduct to supply water to large iron-pans
where it is heated by burning long reeds and
grasses from the hills. Thence it is carried to
tubs in little cubicles made by wooden par-
titions backed by the solid rock.

The Top.* says : "the Monastery of Wa-
" shan Toi was established in 739 A.D. the
" first Buddhist House in this neighbourhood.
" Its name is derived from the tradition that
" once upon a time five hundred Lo-han (the
" Arhat or Disciples of Shakyamuni) with
" variegated heads. (that is, heads of different
" shapes and colours like flowers,) came and
" stopped here. At the end of the XVI.
" century this Monastery became a celebrated
" centre of Buddhist teaching and priests
" flocked here in such numbers that the build-
" ing had to be enlarged. Behind the temple

* There is a Topography of the Lo-fou Mountains,
dating from early in the last century, of which a reprint
can be bought in Canton. It is in ten volumes very
discursive and badly digested as such works usually are,
being more a collection of extracts than a reasoned discourse.
This work is referred to below as Top.

" there are two rocks leaning towards one
" another and meeting at the top like hands
" joined in prayer."

After the caged life of Canton this twenty-
mile walk in heavy rain and wind (a typhoon
was raging in Hongkong) tired us greatly, so
we decided to postpone one day the climb to
the top. In the morning we strolled round
the hill to the East about three miles as far
as the Taoist Monastery Wong-lung Kun
(黃 龍 觀 , meaning Temple of the Yellow
Dragon, situated in a break in the hills amongst
beautiful trees. Just before reaching the
Temple we noticed two priests gathering fruit
from a tree apparently of the orange family,
called by the natives " Nien-ya-Ch'ü " (拈芽桔
The fruit, something between an orange and
a mangostine was strange to us: we sent
specimens to Mr. C. Ford, the Superintendent
of the Botanical Department, Hongkong, but he
was unable to identify the tree. The priests
said the tree only grew in these hills. This
is scarcely likely to be so; however the fruit
appears not to be known in Canton.

This temple contains many rooms but
the space is too much cut up so that guests'
quarters would be rather confined. The Priest
who received us was a very worldly-minded
individual whose heart seemed to be mainly
set on making money: he tried to trade with
us in various lines from mountain tea of
extraordinary virtues and fragrance to pre-

served sweets and orchids, offering to board
and lodge us and our friends, call for orders
in Hongkong and so on.

The Top, refers to the Cave of the Yellow
Dragon (黃 龍 洞), but no mention is made
of this temple, so that we may take it to be
a modern establishment.

Having returned to lunch at Wa-shau
Toi, two of us started to walk to Fa-shan Tze,
which we now discovered to be the temple
passed yesterday at the foot of the mountain,
on a curious mission. One of the last
foreigners who had visited these mountains
was Mr. C. Ford, of Hongkong, in 1883. He
had put up at Fa-shan Tze for the night and
had left four dollars in his host's debt, which
sum he had sent back from the next stage
by the hands of a servant. He had since
discovered that the servant had embezzled the
money, which Mr. Ford had never had an
opportunity of making good until he heard
of our party. Alas! the good old Priest who
had entertained Mr. Ford in 1883 was dead;
but we handed the money to his successor
and explained the reason why it had remained
so long unpaid—much to the astonishment of
the villagers who stood round and listened to
our palaver. This temple is without interest.
It is situated on flat ground and its inmates
seem given up to agriculture. No one should
halt here in summer, but those intending to
climb the mountain should call here for a

guide, as the top temple is the property of this house so that there is constant communication between the two.

On the 20th September, at 9.30 a.m., we started from Wa-shau Toi to climb the mountain. The walking was good and easy sometimes on a firm earth road and sometimes on a roughly made stone path. There was no human abode of any kind between Wa-shau Toi and the top and scarcely a tree between the precincts of the two temples that made the stage. It was an easy climb in point of gradient but the rain poured without ceasing, and, being quite out of training we began by noon to feel the approaches of hunger, indeed one of us said he must eat or he could not go another step. Luckily, at this crisis, one of our porters came up, in whose load we found a tin of cooking raisins of which short work was made. At 2 p.m. we found ourselves on a narrow col (3,950 feet) with precipices on either side. This we took to be the basis of all the fanciful invention about a so-called Iron Bridge* (鐵橋) con-

---

* The common legend is that this range consists of two masses of mountain Lo on the S.W. and Fou on the N.E. Lo is a common sound and name in Chinese, and this mountain is said always to have stood where it is; but Fou, which means "floating," is said to have floated here from P'êng-lai—Fairy-land—somewhere in the Eastern Sea and to be now joined to Lo by the "Iron Bridge." The books say that even now the flora of Fou is marine and that the water in its tarns rises and falls with the tide!

necting the Lo mountain to the Fon of which
so much is said in Chinese books.

From this point we skirted the top of the
mountain leaving it on our left ; descended
some hundred feet ; continued about two miles
on fairly level paths ; went down some hundred
feet and up again having crossed a deep gully
in the heart of the mountains ; rallied on a little
plateau ; and saw through the clouds fifty yards
ahead of us the little Buddhist Temple Put-
wan Tze (撥雲寺) Cloud-dispersing Temple,
—our destination—into which we straggled
one after another about 3 p.m. very glad to get
under shelter from the remorseless rain. The
distance from Wa-shan Toi to Put-wan Tze
is thirteen to fourteen miles. Under favorable
conditions the ascent ought to be done in five
and the descent in four hours : so that men in
condition could get to the top and back easily
in one day.

When a tub, dry clothes, a good lunch and
a cigar had sufficiently stimulated thought and
observation, we became gradually aware that
we shared with certain wooden images a
tumble-down little building standing at a
height of 3,520 feet and at a distance of
fourteen miles from its nearest neighbour. It
was agreeable to find that we were seated
under a water-tight roof at double the height
of the Hongkong Peak in a temp. of 66° Fahr.
on 20th September : the more so that we had
brought up with us dry clothes, blankets,

bread, ham, claret, coffee and whiskey; and
who could want more at the moment?

This temple may perhaps be described
with some detail as its strange situation is
likely to make it interesting to other Europeans
visiting these mountains, although it has no
intrinsic merit. The main building consists
of three rooms alongside, with broken-down
out-houses at right angles on either hand, so
as to form three sides of a square. The
Western room does duty as Principal Hall
and here is the usual gilt wooden Image of
Buddha—we wished to put up our camp beds
here but found that it leaked. The middle
room is very small and is moreover encum-
bered by a stone altar. Behind this room is
a loft, where the Botanical Collectors sent
with us by Mr. C. Ford put up. The Eastern
room, which is much the best, measures
about 18 feet by 25 feet and has a tiled
floor. In the place of honour is an Image
of the Instructor in Medicine, Buddha, a
god with an incense-burner in front and
a lamp to light at night consisting of a
foreign glass tumbler half full of oil with
a piece of pith hanging over the side as wick.
During our stay the worship of this Deity
had to be suspended as our beds took up the
whole space: but in lieu thereof he heard a
lot of discussion and argument. This temple
was built in 1868. The only curious thing
about it, is that the two Eastern rooms

are roofed with foreign corrugated iron. A
traveller coming on the temple suddenly would
probably find but one man in occupation with
rice and very little else. There is a garden
with a few herbs. There was one domestic
creature only—a cock—who was supported for
religious purposes. Finding he was not for
sale and that there was no chance of getting
him into our larder, we felt truly grieved for
his lonely condition: indeed one of our number,
who was undergoing a course of medicine, occasionally threw him a pill which he swallowed
with confidence! During the clear weather of
October, November and December this Temple
would be a paradise to a small party of
sportsmen or botanists, well provided with
the necessaries of western life.

On the next day, 21st September, we
started under the guidance of the Priest to
visit a place called Ku-yu Toi (古遙臺),
Enchanting Terrace of the Ancients. We
walked through mist and rain down gorges,
across valleys, fording streams, trying to
emulate the career of flies on a wall, with
no track—excepting wild-boar runs—and nothing but the guidance of the Priest to keep
us together in the mist—on and on for about
an hour in a direction a little North of East
from the temple. At last we found ourselves
on a small terrace covered with grass and
flowers but bare of trees; and stretching below
us a most magnificent view worth all our

pains since leaving Canton. The main ridge
of the mountains ran away to the North East:
below us was a sheer and apparently imprac-
ticable descent: the valley was clothed in
stately virgin forest—as inaccessible, our
guide said, from below as from where we
stood, above. My mind does not recall
accurately, nor if it did could I find words
to express, the effect of what we saw
by glimpses as the mist rose and fell: the
perfect rest and stillness, the noble forest,
the vast expanse beginning with the giant
trees beneath us, then the steep sides of the
mountain, then the outlying hills, then the
broad plain with the hazy shape of mountains
beyond on the horizon. And there was not a
vestige of man or of his work—stout Cortez
upon a peak in Darien could not have seen
less.

There is a tradition that this remote forest
is peopled by monkeys; hear what Dr. B. C.
Henry says in his excellent work " Ling-nam "
page 317: " from this terrace (Ku-yu Toi)
" we look down into the mysterious depths
" of Monkey Gorge, an inaccessible ravine
" covered with a dense growth of trees and
" shrubs, and inhabited by a large tribe of
" monkeys. Guarded from below by a sheer
" precipice, which no one has yet been able
" to climb, and from above by an equally
" precipitous descent, which no one has dared
" to attempt, its depths are yet unexplored,

" and the monkeys left in undisturbed posses-
" sion. A stone hurled from above into the
" tree tops brings them out in angry remons-
" trance against such insults. Living on the
" wild fruits and nuts of their mountain
" retreat, they seem to have sufficient food,
" except in times of drought or extreme cold,
" when they issue forth in search of susten-
" ance. Numerous tales of their depredations
" are told. On one occasion they made a
" descent upon the orchard of the Pak-hok
" monastry, and in a single night stripped
" it of an abundant crop of various fruits, a
" trail of seeds and shells leading up the hill
" showing who the marauders were. An old
" priest at Put-wan had many tales to tell
" about them, and seemed to think them
" almost human. He had watched them at
" play, and seen the parents toss the little
" ones back and forth between them like
" balls. Companies of three hundred have
" been seen at one time."

Dr. Henry, you will observe, does not say
that he saw these monkeys himself: gladly,
no doubt, accepting the picturesque effect that
the image of monkeys tossing their babies
about among the trees of the forest primeval
adds to his pages, he refers the reader to a
native of the Gorgeous East as his authority.
This was wisely done; but a British youth
of Canton went further, and informed one of
us that he had seen these monkeys with his

own eyes. This was why we had burdened
ourselves with " fallible rifle and devious shot
gun," and why we now sat down and waited
on this ancient bowling-green, ready for attack
or defence, and watching carefully for a
glimpse of our interesting first cousins, whom
we imagined well advanced in the evolutionary
ascent. But we were disappointed; not a
vestige of monkeys did we see; and my own
opinion is that these monkeys like the " Iron
Bridge," the ancient musical instruments referred to below and so many other wonders of
these hills are only visible to the eye of faith,
that is to say they have no objective existence.

On the 23rd September, Dr. Wales and
I determined to retrace our steps as far as
the col mentioned in describing our ascent,
and thence to climb Fi-wang-ting (飛雲頂),
Flying-cloud Summit, the highest peak in
these mountains.

We reached the col without event and a
short climb of a couple of hundred feet or so
towards the W.N.W. brought us to the top.
We stayed there about half an hour in order
to take a careful reading of pressure and tem-
perature for altitude: corrected, they are as
follows; 1892, 23rd September, 1 p.m. 63° Fahr.
25.85 inches. This worked out with the
Hongkong Observatory as the Lower Station
gives 4,150 feet as the height of the mountain.
On the occasion of my second visit to Lo-fou,
I made at the same place the following obser-

vations : 1894. January 11th, 10 a.m. 52° Fahr.
26.03 inches which worked out in the same
way gives the height as 4,120.

We may therefore with some confidence
put the height of the Lo-fou Mountains at
about 4,150 feet above the sea level.

Near the top stands a stone altar to
the God of the Lo-fou Mountains, the Deity
who is imagined to have charge of the govern-
ment of this District. The inscription is—

粵　嶽　祠

羅浮君尊神位

香山黃培芳題
南海廖翔敬書

Close by we were astonished to find an ordinary
grave with an inscription dated 1839 to the
effect that this was the tomb of the Honoured
Wife, whose maiden surname was Ho, of Ch'ên
(陳), of the village of Mu-yuan (穆 院), who
represented the 17th generation of his family.
Probably the bones were collected some years
after death and brought here.

The view from Fi-wang Ting must be
magnificent when the air is clear, but we were

in clouds and could scarcely see the plain at
all. On the occasion of my second visit in
January, 1894, the weather was cold and the
air appeared clear, as it really was in the
upper regions, but below, the features of the
landscape were shrouded in a fine mist rising
from—

"......those dim fields about the homes

"Of happy men......

"And grassy barrows of the happier dead."

For an extended view one should be here on
a clear humid day in spring. The Top. says :
" Fi-wang Ting is the highest peak of the Lo
" Mountain and stands erect to Heaven. In
" fine weather there is a mist below. The
" Philosopher Chu (朱子) often climbed this
" peak in the early morning to see the tops of
" the neighbouring peaks emerge from the mist
" as if from a sea. As the clouds roll past,
" one feels as if the mountain were moving—a
" curious sensation." Lakes and pagodas are
then mentioned but of these we saw nothing :
however if the Philosopher Chu got here in
the early morning there must have been a
building of some sort up here unless he was
even greater as a mountaineer than as a
Philosophical Critic. Then the Top. drags in
"the Iron Bridge" and says : " there are two
" solitary peaks standing detached and oppo-
" site each other. This bridge connects them ;
" but being built of stones like those of which
" a rainbow is formed, it is seldom seen ! "

We were walking back to our temple wondering why Ch'ên sent his Wife's bones to such an extraordinary resting place, and had concluded that it must have been ambition for his descendants based on fêng-shui, when we started a wild-boar from the gully below us about a hundred yards off. It scuttled off up the glen along side our path, stopping several times almost broadside on towards us. Unfortunately we carried nothing more deadly than umbrellas and aneroid barometers; so he went his way in peace.

On the 24th September our party broke up, Doctors Wales and Atkinson and Mr. Badeley returning to Canton by the way we had come; while Mr. Wyon and myself started further into the mountains. We had been very unlucky in the weather at Put-wan Tze for we were in rain and mist the whole time. We would have stayed a day or two longer in the hope of seeing the sun, but our servants were doubled up by the cold and we had to descend to a warmer level or have sick men on our hands.

II.—PUT-WAN TZE TO SU-LIU KUN.

Therefore at 11 a.m. we said good-bye to our kind old Host and the rough but well-meant hospitality of Put-wan, and made our way North by a pathway giving grand views of a range of mountains on the N.W. After half an hour's walk we came upon a meadow about a hundred yards square that had evidently been levelled by man and that bore traces of former buildings. The spot is known as Siao-teen mun (小天門) Little Heaven's Gate. The view towards the North was now very fine; in fact one is here on the Northern edge of the main plateau of the mountain. One can walk quite up to the edge of the plateau where a stream falls shear over the rocks splashing down one precipice after another for about 2,000 feet. Far away below us in the valley stands a circular hill, clothed on one side with a splendid grove of fir trees, the dark green of whose foliage contrasts well with the lighter greens and reds on the slopes around. Our guide informed us that in front of this grove was situated the Taoist Monastery Su-liu Kun, our present destination. At Little Heaven's Gate the serious descent began and remarkably steep it was by a zig-zaging clay pathway made very slippery by fallen leaves. The changing panorama of light and shade over the crater-shaped valley below us was enchanting. The rocks that border the torrent are covered with orchids. After a descent of two to three thousand feet we reached fairly level ground with a wood-cutter's shelter and an occasional tree (1,200 feet). Here we met two separate parties of men, 5 or 6 in each, out after wild boar. Their method apparently was to burn out a patch on the hill side and shoot what came out of it. As we follow the stream further North we get lovely glimpses of the waterfall which can be traced for the whole of its course of 2,000 feet. Softened by distance the broken crags and gullies over which we have just come look like a green expanse.

At 4 p.m. we reached Su-liu Kun* (酥醪觀)—a place that did not belie our high expectations. The buildings are spacious and in excellent order; and the site is well chosen. The temple itself is strongly built and richly adorned: the magnificent fir trees, the mere with large boulders placed in semi-circles above its banks, on which the priests sit to chat and survey the landscape; the perfect calm and sylvan beauty of the surroundings; and above all the discipline and order that reigned amongst the inmates of this House struck us with something like astonishment.

---

* Note that Kun is a Taoist and Tze a Buddhist Temple.

The meaning of the name Su Liu is rather vague; but it undoubtedly points to Wine and Wine-bibbing. Su (蘇) probably meant a fermented drink made from milk; and Liu (醪) means lees of wine. Probably the two characters are best rendered in English by nectar, mountain dew or some such poetic name. Several paintings on the walls of the temple record exploits with the bottle; altogether it seems that Taoism contains in its heterogeneous divine répertoire some counterpart of Bacchus.

We were received by a most affable and courteous individual, arrayed in Taoist garb, who, without speaking a word that we could understand, made us clearly aware of his high consideration and distinguished sentiments towards us. He struck attitudes, threw his gown around, and deported himself like a pea-cock. His special duty, we afterwards learned, is to receive and to provide for the comfort of guests.

The "Pea-cock" allotted us excellent quarters with a large court-yard to ourselves. at the back of which was a newly-built and gorgeously painted hall, fifty feet by thirty.

We were given a particularly warm welcome by an old Priest whose real name is Li P'ing Lu, who assumed the name of Chih-p'ing (至平)—Peace attained—on entering religion. He spoke English fluently, telling us that he had passed many years in San

Francisco where he was cook in a French
Restaurant. He had come here to pass the
remainder of his days. He was not a regular
priest but a lay-brother. He had paid a lump
sum to the Temple on entering and was
provided with food and shelter till he died.
His only duties were to wash and brush the
Images of the Gods every morning at day-
break and to brew early tea for the Priests—
then his work was over for the day. What
a contrast to the life of a cook in a San
Francisco Restaurant!

Another who had forgotten most of his
English had been for many years a merchant
in the United States. He had returned to
China in bad health. He knew his heart was
weak and he could not stand the wear and
tear of active trade. He had some money
and debated with himself whether he should
take a wife. "If I married I said to myself
" I might have a son—that would be good:
" but then I might not have a son, and there
" are serious troubles and drawbacks." He
decided that he would retire to this temple
and end his days in peace here. Men lived
here longer than elsewhere because of the
excellence of the air and water.

Exact discipline is maintained at this
temple—that is as such things go in China.
The drum is beaten and the doors shut at sun-
down. A regular service of drum-beating
and chanting is gone through twice a day—at

dawn and dusk. The shooting and snaring of birds and the cutting of wood is strictly forbidden, and to this end the grove of fir trees behind the temple is guarded day and night by an old man living in a mat-shed, in the middle of the wood, who, by the way, addressed us in English, telling us that he had formerly been employed in Hongkong.

The result is that the wood resounds day and night with the call of birds rarely heard in China. In the stillness of the night this is very remarkable. Kites, owls, &c. innumerable keep up a constant clatter by day and put in a shriek every few minutes at night

In regard to Natural History, I can do little more than recommend to the notice of Hongkong Botanists this district—especially the country around Siu-Liu Kun—as abounding in flowering shrubs, creepers, grasses and ferns. The district has never been investigated by a competant man on the spot: Mr. C. Ford, of Hongkong, came here, it is true. but he made but a flying visit. The native collectors whom Mr. Ford sent with us on this trip made a collection, which is now under examination. but they were far from learned in classification —they divided the flora into two classes only, namely "Hongkong side have got" and "Hongkong side no got." Doubtless they left those which they ought to have taken and took those which they ought to have left; for there was very little botanical health in them.

So far there have been found among the plants we gathered one new genus namely Gesneraceæ, Didymocarpeæ. Bournea Sinensis (Oliv.) named after the Writer (see Hooker's Icones Plantarum, Part III., May, 93); and one new species, Compositaceæ, Carpesium Atkinsonianum (Helms.) named after Dr. Atkinson. Of the other plants collected a list will be found in Appendix (D). We noticed growing wild at Su-liu, Lantana, Marigold, Chrysanthemum and Clerodendron squamatium : tea oil and *t'ung* oil trees are here much culitvated. There seems to be a considerable trade in medicinal herbs, roots, &c., from these hills, as well as in weird shaped walking sticks and other "natural curiosities," so called apparently because in an inanimate object a resemblance is found to something in the animate world : for instance the root of a fern does duty for a deer—four fronds are cut off so that their bases form legs, the hairy covering looks like fur, and the stock, from which both roots and fronds spring, is the body, the *tout ensemble* often bearing an odd likeness. The following herb amongst others was being collected : 菖蒲 ? Acorus calamus.

I must not forget two very different forms of life—butterflies and oxen—battleships and canoes of the animal world—possessing only one thing in common—the power to support themselves for a season above the level of the dull inanimate. The number and beauty of

the butterflies in these hills is astonishing.
We noticed many varieties round Su-lui, but
I can only describe one, which was of steel
blue with light coloured facings. We saw as
many as twenty of this species together—a
gorgeous spectacle. Indeed these mountains
are renowned for butterflies: there is a Butter-
fly Gorge (蝴蝶洞) which appears from
the map in the Top. to be above and to the
North of Ch'ung-hü Kun (see page 31) and in
regard to which the Top. says: "It has been
" handed down that the Immortal Kê Hung's
" clothes, discarded as he ascended to Heaven,
" were turned into butterflies." The oxen in
these parts are of a small but remarkably
sleek and well-shaped breed, and seem to be
more used for field work here than buffaloes.
They are all muzzled in a very simple and
effective way, the muzzle being made of
bamboo.

Su-lui Kun was built in the reign of
K'ang-hi (1662—1723) as an off-shoot of
Ch'ung-hü Kun. It was repaired in the
sixties and is now in excellent order. We
were told that all the land in the neighbourhood had formerly belonged to the temple
and that it had now a long rent-roll.

The Images of the Gods worshiped in
this Temple are displayed in the usual way.
In the main hall there are three Images: Lei
Tsu (雷祖), the Patriarch Thunder; Lü
Tsu (呂祖) the Patriarch Lü—(呂洞賓)

born A.D. 755, a Taoist Doctor supposed to
have been a great proficient in the black art
and now much worshiped by the sick; and
Kô Tsu (葛 祖)—Kô Hung al. Chih-ch'uan
(葛 洪 字 稚 川), a local celebrity of whom
we shall have much more to say. He was
one of the most renowned among the Doctors
of Taoism and adepts in the art and practice
of alchemy. He is said to have attained to
the state of immortality and his disappearance
from earth at the age of 81 is reported about
A.D. 330*

This hall is decorated with careful paintings
of events in Taoist legend. In a separate
chapel to the left of the main hall there stands
a shrine with an image of Kuan-yin, the
Buddhist Goddess of Mercy! To find this
in a Taoist Temple might astonish a new-
comer from Europe, but the fact is quite
in accordance with Chinese practice. No
man hath seen God at any time: so that
the idea of God cannot be exactly the same
in any two human minds. If the adherents
of one creed find in another creed an idea
or mental image of a Deity embracing
qualities and attributes which they admire,
why should they not worship that God?
The idea is everything: the name nothing.
Supernatural religion is concerned solely with

---

* See Mayers' "Chinese Reader's Manual," page 87.

the subjective.* So think the Chinese: such
thinking is reasonable but it does not make
martyrs or patriots.

While we were at Su-lui we noticed
almost every day new faces—pilgrims just
arrived some of them young and intelligent
looking. There seems to be a continuous
stream of these traveling priests. It is hard
to see a sufficient object to attract them up
and down the land from temple to temple.
There are no schools to visit or lectures to
attend—the great attraction to travel in the
Middle Ages in Europe. Such pilgrimages
are probably a tradition from early Buddhism,
copied by Taoism. The leading idea seems
to be that there is advantage and merit in
visiting celebrated shrines and in seeing the
marvels of nature that surround them—as if
what were rare, beautiful, awful or grotesque
in nature lay closer to the Gods than do the
common objects of daily life. Is it for the same
reason that man all over the world has placed
upon hills the Temples of the Gods? or is it
more correct to view the question from the
side of those Celestial Beings and to imagine
with the late E. C. Baber, that the Gods
prefer to live on hills in order to escape far

---

* A Confucian Commentator puts this very clearly
(see An. 3, 12): "If a man sacrifices in sincerity there is
" a God (or spirit); if not in sincerity, there is no God
" (or spirit)."

from man, whose company they find very fatiguing?*

But to return to our three Images—the God of Thunder, that is, the Imaginery Official who is supposed to command Heaven's artillery and two Medical Praditioners who dealt in simples, magic and alchemy. The trio equally enjoy the title of Ancestor or Patriarch, and each has a wooden Image. Does not the reader think them rather an ill-assorted Trinity, and wonder what Taoism really is? We must try to answer him, as he has been indulgent enough to come with us so far.

In early Chinese records we find many references to the worship of Supernatural Beings, the Emperor worships Heaven, the People worship the Gods of each particular spot of land; Mountains and Streams are worshiped, and the Spirits of Departed Men. In fact the Chinese seem always to have been free—as they now are—to picture in their minds and worship just what Supernatural Beings they chose. There was then in the Chinese mind, as there is now, a vague image of a Supernatural World consisting of countless

---

* E. C. Baber told the Writer that, being asked to contribute something to the Album of the Great Temple on Mount Omi in Ssu-ch'uan on the borders of Thibet, he wrote :—

The Gods of Greek, of Hebrew and of Jew
Lived on Olympus Horeb and Meru ;
The Gods of Omi have the self-same plan
And live as far as possible from man.

Beings who were behind and controlled pheno-
mena. The Chief of these Beings was called
Shang-ti, the Supreme God, who seems to have
been pictured as ruling the Supernatural
World much as the Feudal Lord or Emperor
ruled the Kingdoms of which China then
consisted. To this state of things came Con-
fucius who summed up the practical philosophy
and ethics of the day and occupied with his
teaching the sphere of human relations—
man's duty to his neighbour—but left the
rest much as he found it. Then followed
Buddhism from India and occupied the sphere
of man's relations to a future life, with fixed
tenets and teaching. in fact a Religion—and
the first China had heard of. That she had
no religion of her own is proved by the fact
that she has no word with that meaning, *kiao*
the word in use. meaning no more than
"doctrine." *Taoism was the attempt of the
native scholars to make out of the heterogeneous
materials of Nature-Worship a religion after the
model of, and to serve as a rival to, Buddhism.*
That is why our three Gods are such an ill-
assorted team.

But to the above a correction must be
applied, tending however to make the subject
matter of Taoism more mixed still. There is
(1) Lao Tzŭ's teaching about *Tao, the way;*
and there is (2) the Black Art, the search for
the elixir of life and the philosopher's stone—
these two have both been important elements

in Taoism and cannot be disregarded. The second requires no explanation. Chinese alchemy seems to have followed much the same course as in the West. In regard to *Tao* we will venture a word of explanation for it is far the most important term in Chinese philosophy and seems to embrace a valuable idea. What does it mean? *The way or right course.* But whither? Suppose the universe of mind and matter to be subject to immutable forces and laws from the effects of which man has absolutely no hope of escape; and suppose a man contemplates doing something whether with his hands or with his brain, there is one best way to effect his object and that *best way* is *Tao*. It is true that the word is often very vaguely used but in its abstract sense it usually means either (1) the immutable laws of the universe themselves when it corresponds to *natura* of the Stoics* or (2) the right way to act with regard to those laws as explained above.

Clearly this idea of *Tao* is for the learned, and alchemy being long ago dead, there remains only Nature-worship—and that is what Taoism is for the mass of the people. Indeed I believe we may go much further and say that the worship of Nature and An-cestors is the fundamental religious idea in

---

* See Watters' learned disquisition on this word " Essays in the Chinese Language," page 229.

the Chinese mind now as it was two thousand
years ago, and that foreign religions have
been very ill assimilated by the national
thought—they are hooked on from the outside
and show no organic growth. The Catechism
taught us to distinguish duty to God and duty
to one's neighbour: in China Nature · and
Ancestor worship regulate the first, and Con-
fucianism the second.

On the 28th September, we walked to
Ch'a-shan Kun, (茶 山 觀), the Temple of
the Tea Hill, subsidiary to Su-liu, situated at
the top of a break in the hills amongst fine
trees, 1,300 feet above the sea. The air was
loaded with the fragrance of flowers and fruit:
in the court-yard there was a fine *olea fragrans*
in flower, and in front of the temple carambola
and pulemo trees covered with yellow fruit—
a garden of the Hesperides.

III.—Su-liu Kun by way of Ch'ung-hü Kun to Canton.

On the 29th September, we left Su-liu after a pleasant stay of five days. Our porters. engaged for us by one of the priests, gave no trouble, and at 9 a.m. we were under weigh bound for Ch'ung-hü Kun. (冲虚觀), the Temple of Aerial Ascent. We followed the Ch'a-shan Kun road till we reached a rest-house on the top of the pass, just above that temple, whence we began the descent—towards the S.S.E. After a couple of miles of steepish gradient, we left the mountains behind us (220 feet) and passed the day amongst hills some-times well-wooded, but commonplace after the magnificent scenery we had left. At 2 p.m. we reached Ch'ung-hü, our destination—celebrated as the oldest establishment at Lo-fou and as the abode of Kê Hung, the Taoist Immortal of whom I have already spoken. and the place from which he ascended to Heaven. The temple buildings are of most solid con-struction. In front—on the South—is. as usual. a D-shaped mere or fish pond; between this and the main entrance a broad terrace paved with blocks of stone; a massive stone *perron* leads to the doors opposite which in the entrance-hall stands an image of Kê Hung; and then comes a minor hall or chapel forming the southern side of a spacious concreted terrace about 120 by 60 feet with dwelling rooms on either side and the main hall at the top—the North. All the buildings are raised four feet above the ground on large well-cut blocks of stone. The temple was last rebuilt or repaired on a large scale (重 修) in 1666. The more perishable parts—wood-work, roofing, tiles, paint, &c., are in very bad order, but the stone and concrete is almost untouched by time. The main hall is a melancholy sight; it is in such a dangerous condition that it has had to be closed till money can be raised for its repair. Through the broken windows we could see the three Taoist Gods, each with his face wrapped in yellow paper that he might be saved the spectacle of desolation around him.

We were much disappointed in this temple. From Chinese books we had been led to expect some genuine relics of antiquity here. We had read of primitive musical instruments made of stone that were preserved here. The oldest priest we could find said he had heard of such things but had never seen them—there were none now.

Having engaged a priest as guide we set out next morning to see the "wonders" for which this temple is famous. About 20 yards from the back wall he pointed to the side of the hill and said, "That is where the Immortal "Kê took the earth out of which he made the

" Elixir of Life." Where? we asked, for the hill-side looked like any other, overgrown with spear-grass and scrub. He replied. "Only Immortals can distinguish the spot." This startled us: we were getting deep into theology.

The next wonder, so-called, was a grave-stone on which were clearly cut the following characters (衣冠塚) meaning Tomb of the Clothes and Hat. A stone is said to have been erected here in the Sung Period (A.D. 960—1278) and replaced by this one in the reign of K'ien-lung (A.D. 1736—1796). After Kê Hung had taken the Elixir of Life and felt that he was on his way aloft, just as he passed this place, he divested himself of his hat and clothes: only when he felt his feet well above the ground, did he discard his boots, to which there is a separate grave higher up the hill.

There are many more wonders but no doubt the reader has had enough. Not far off is the Pak-hok Kun (白鶴觀) a large Taoist Temple that we had no time to visit.

To the South of Ch'ung-hü is a village named Mei-hua Ts'un (梅花村) Plum-blossom Village. The Top. says: about the end of the sixth century A.D. a statesman named Chao Shih-hsiung (趙師雄) who had been banished to these parts, "in the cool of " the evening being at a wine-shop in a " pine wood somewhat drunk saw a woman

淺
雪
未
消

? ?

translat...

? ?

" approaching dressed in every-day clothes.
" He went out to meet her it being then dusk
" with a glimmer of light from the moon.
" He talked to her and was captivated. While
" they were drinking together a youth dressed
" in green laughed, danced and sang before
" them. Chao, being drunk, slept. Gradually
" he began to feel a penetrating cold air;
" 'twas already light in the East; he rose and
" found himself underneath a plum tree on
" which was perched a bird with bright blue
" (kingfisher-like) plumage, singing loudly.
" The moon had set; the morning star had
" risen; and Chao felt dull and dejected."

The sites are shown of two ancient buildings connected with this enterprising statesman for whose banishment there was probably good cause.

There is so much about these mountains in Chinese literature, the existing temples are so extensive and ruins attest so clearly a great part of their glory to have departed, that one wonders whether the richer classes in China were once more active physically than they are now? Was there ever a genuine spirit of exploration and enquiry among the richer classes or have they always given their brains, in youth to the mental gymnastics of essay and verse making, and in maturer age to the delicate operation of extorting all the money possible from the pockets of the people without causing rebellion—as they do now? Did

the vanguard of the Chinese camp always
consist of washermen and cabbage growers,
driven forth from their native villages by the
inexorable law of Malthus, and never of youths
led to go abroad by the longing for fresh
fields and pastures new?

In the present day a few young men
come to these hills to study and a few old
men for change of air when sickness has over-
taken them, and there are some decent looking
itinerant priests mentioned above; but the
majority of the inmates of these temples are
idle, mangy, loafing priests and criminals
escaped from justice. Three students from
Su-lin succeeded at the metropolitan examination in 1891, one taking the third place
(探花), a very high honour. On the other
hand it was in hiding at the desolate ruined
buildings of Ch'ung-hü Kun, whither he had
gone for his health, that Lo Hok-pang, late
Compradore of the Hongkong and Shanghai
Bank, died.

The Top: gives some descriptions of the
mountains written in the T'ang (618—905)
and Sung (960—1278) Dynasties that smack
of a personal visit, and there is one by P'an
Lei (潘耒) dated about the end of the XVII
century that is racy and vigorous and suggests
physical activity; but then there are others
of the same date that are typically Chinese.
in which the author reveals himself clearly
sitting at home concocting in polished phrases

fancy pictures in which every thing is con-
ventional. Coming down to the beginning
of the last century the Chinese appear to have
been much as they are now in this respect.
The Top: rejoices in seven prefaces. the first
by the Canton Viceroy of 1717 beginning as
follows : "The universe contained Titanic
" gases which condensed into rivers and
" solidified into mountains—some so large
" as to be the cynosure of a country side. I
" know by report the fame of the Lo-fou
" Mountains, but have never been able to
" visit them" and so on. Then follow six
other prefaces written each by a Canton
official of that year, of the utmost dulness
distinguished from one another only by the
type in which they are printed. But one
significant statement they one and all make
" *that the Writer had not himself visited the*
" *Mountains.*" Considering the ecstatic admi-
ration they profess to feel, and that they were
living only 50 miles off, they were probably of
much the same kidney as their successors of
to-day. What these gentry are like we all
know. Here is an example : a year or two ago
the Commissioner sent down from Peking to
examine for Official Degrees happened to pass
these mountains on his circuit and to be
carried through Mei-hua Ts'un, Plum-blossom
Village. Now it happens that this village is
often mentioned in Chinese literature as rich in
plum trees. The Examiner put his head out

of his chair and asked where he was? "This
is Plum-blossom Village your Excellency."
" Where then are the Plum-tree groves," asked
he. There were none : a thousand years having
passed, they were naturally dead. The
polished Literatus did not get out of his chair
but his spirit was deeply moved. On his
return to Canton he raised a subscription to
have the Plum-tree groves replanted. He
objected to have his settled beliefs disturbed
or to readjust his thoughts if it could be
helped.

On the 1st October, we walked from
Ch'ung-hü to Kao-tsai T'ong (狗仔塘) on a
tributary of the East River, a distance of
about 13 miles, passing a temple named Pou-
tsick Tze (寶積寺) some mile or more on
our right. The only place to put up in is a
benevolent establishment (體仁堂) hot, dirty
and fly-blown, and it was with much satis-
faction that soon after day-light next morning
we went on board shallow boats that carried us
down to Shek-lung in between two and three
hours : there our launch was waiting for us
and at 4 p.m. on the 2nd October, we were
again off Shamien.

IV.—Second Trip—by way of Tsang-shing.

Reference has been made in the above narrative to a second trip to the Lo-fou Mountains, of which, as the range was then attacked from another direction, a short note may be made. On the 4th January, 1894, the writer started from Canton in company with Mr. H. Bent. On the morning of the 5th January, we entered the Tsang-shing River— a tributary of the East River which for the first few miles traverses a plain where we found snipe and doves but nothing better. Higher up, the hills on the river's left bank look very likely cover but we found nothing in them. The scenery now becomes very beautiful. The river is perfectly clear its blue water running over a bed of white sand, bordered by old knarled Chinese olive-trees (Canarium) whose dark green leaves and white bark strike the eye. Tsang-shing 增城 is a quiet country town with a well-to-do peasantry, that treated us with much civility. A few miles above the town we met a fine old man sitting under a tree, a servant holding his pony by his side. He told us that he had several times been on pilgrimages to the top of Lo-fou. His pony—a remarkably well-bred looking animal, smaller boned and more graceful than the Mongolian—was, he

told us, bred in the Lung-mên District on the
N.E. We passed several men carrying skins
of Yeh-li (野 狸)? wild cat—going down
from Ching kuo to Canton to be made into
Chinese writing pencils.

We had a strong N.E. gale against us
which greatly retarded our big flat-bottomed
native boat (Ho-tao) and we only reached
Ching-kuo, about 40 miles from the mouth
of the river, at 3.30 p.m. on the 7th inst.—
a little town traversed by the river along a
broad bed of bright sand, and shut in on the
North and West by mountains.

It took us about seven hours to walk
from Ching-kuo to Su-liu Kun, through hilly
country the whole way. The hills round the
monastery were now (January) covered with
shrubs of every variety of brown, yellow and
green, apparently splendid cover, but unfortunately, at the time of our visit, bare of game.
We and our dogs beat the cover for hours,
but saw no game whatever; probably there
never is much, indeed the birds of prey
protected in the trees behind the temple
would be alone enough to keep down the
head of game; but perhaps we may partly
attribute our bad luck to the unusual dryness of
the season—a phenomenon that is believed by
natives to have been the cause of the out-break
in Canton of bubonic plague the same month.

On the 10th January we walked up from
Su-liu to Put-wan in $3\frac{3}{4}$ hours. On the plateau

at the top we saw a couple of partridge and very abundant marks of wild boar in all directions; but our leave being up we could not stay to look for them. Our min. thermometer marked 33° Fahr. during the night, and there was plenty of ice in exposed places. This was on the 10th January with a South wind, the minimum in Hongkong being 52°. The next day we walked down from Put-wan to Fa-shau Tze in 4½ hours. On the way down we passed lying below us on our right an extensive block of buildings which our guide told us was Nam Miu (藍 廟 —an ancient foundation neither Buddhist nor Taoist. I know nothing more about this temple nor can I find anyone in Canton who has heard of it : whether I misunderstood the guide or whether there really is a large establishment on the S.W. of the range known by the above or some other name, I must leave the next explorer of Lo-fou to discover. The buildings in question, we took to be on about the same level as, and about three miles to the N.W. of, Wa-shan Toi.

From Fa-shau Tze we walked to Kao-tsai Tong where we stayed in the same dirty quarters bothered by the same gaping crowd of ill-kept children.

The next day we went down to Shek-lung in a rapid boat, on from Shek-lung down the East River in a somewhat larger craft and at 10 p.m. we picked up our launch at Sin

Tong (新塘) on the East River, the highest point it could then reach. On the 14th January, at day-light, we were back in Canton.

APPENDIX.

A.—ITINERARY AND MAP.

First Trip.

Canton to Shek-lung 60	miles.
Shek-lung to Wa-shan Toi ...21	,,
Wa-shan Toi to Put-wan Tze ...13	,,
Put-wan Tze to Su-liu Kun ...10	
Su-liu Kun to Ch'ung-hü Kun ...15	.,
Ch'ung-hü Kun to Kao-tsai Tong 13	,,
Kao-tsai Tong to Shek-lung ...12	,,

Second Trip.

Canton to Sin Tong 40	,,
Sin Tong to mouth of Tsang Shing River... 10	,,
Mouth of Tsang-shing River to Ching-kuo 40	,.
Ching-kuo to Su-liu Kun 18	.,
Su-liu Kun to Put-wan Tze ...10	,.
Put-wan Tze to Fa-shan Tze ...16	,,
Fa-shan Tze to Kao-tsai Tong... 8	,,
Kao-tsai Tong to Shek-lung ...12	.,

The Map is intended to give a rough general idea of the lay of the mountains and the relative position of the temples.

B.—ALTITUDES.

These observations were taken with a maximum and a minimum thermometers and two $2\frac{3}{4}''$ pocket aneroids supplied by L. Casella, London, the aneroids being checked by two 1 foot Boiling-point Thermometers by the same maker—all with Kew corrections. The Hongkong Observatory has been taken as the lower station, and the observations worked out by the tables given on pages 286-287 Hints to Travellers, 6th edition. Dr. Doberck, of the Hongkong Observatory. was kind enough to supply the data for the lower station.

No.	DATE.	PLACE.	Mean of observed Pressures Inches.	Mean of observed Temp. Fahr.	Height above sea level	REMARKS.
1	1892 Sept. 18-20	Fa-shan Toi	.. 29,05	77°	580	Mean of 4 observations.
2	„ 20 & 23	Col.	.. 26,05	71	3950	„ 2
3	20-24	Put-wan Tze	.. 26,16	63	3520	„ 7 „
4	„ 23	Fi-wang-ting	.. 25,85	63	4150	
5	24	Little Heaven's gate.	26,67	63	3350	
6	24	Crossing	.. 28,70	73	1200	
7	24-29	su-liu Kun..	.. 29,00	73	810	„ „ 10
8	„ 28	Cha-shan Kun ..	.. 28,62	80	1290	
9	29	Gate	.. 28,62	71	1250	
10	29	Crossing	.. 29,64	71	220	
11	„ „ 29 to Oct. 1	Chung-hii Kun ..	.. 29,86	71	70	„ „ 4
12	1894 Jan. 8-10	su-liu Kun..	.. 29,42	43	810	„ 3
13	10-11	Put-wan Tze	.. 26,60	42	3470	„ 2
14	„ „ 11	Fi-wang-ting	.. 26,03	52	4120	

C.—LATITUDES AND LONGITUDES.

These observations were made with a 6″ sextant and a half Chronometer Watch by Blockley (Kew A Certificate 76·3 marks). They must be taken as approximate only.

Name of Place.	Lat. North.	Long. East.
Su-liu Kun...	... 23° 20′ 30″	114° — —
Put-wan Tze		114° 02′ —
Fa-shan Tze	... 23. 13. —	113. 56 —

COMPARE :—

Hongkong ...	... 22° 16′ 30″	114˚ 09′ 42″
Canton British Consulate...	23. 07′ 35″	113. 15. —

D.—PLANTS COLLECTED.

Of the plants collected, twenty were sent by Mr. C. Ford. Head of the Botanical Dept., Hongkong, to Kew, for identification in 1892. Although we are now in 1895 only two have yet been heard of, namely, Bournea Sinensis and Carpesium Atkinsonianum, mentioned above: all the botanical talent at the command of H. M. Goverment is supposed to be grappling with the other eighteen.

The remaining plants collected were identified by Mr. Ford as follows :—

Podophyllum versipelli, Hance.
Pittosporum glabratum, H. and A.
Hypericum attenuatum, Choicy.
Hibicus syriacus.
Triumfetta pilosa Roth.
Rhamnus crenata S. et Z.
Pueraria Thunbergiana, Benth.
Pueraria phaseoloides, Benth.
Lespedeza? viatorum, Champ.
Atylosia scarabaeoides, Benth.
Flemingia congesta, Roxb.
Sonerila tenera, R. Br.
Osbeckia crinita, Benth.
Melastoma repens, Lam.
Sonerila Fordii, Oliv.
Srichosauthes multiloba, Mig.
Hydrocotyle javanica, Thbj.
Peucedanum decursivum, Max.
Œnanthe stolonifera, D. C.

Ophiorhiza pumila, Champ.
Hedyotis boerhaavioides, Hance.
Hedyotis acutangula Bth.
Hedyotis hispida, Retz.
Poederia Tomentosa, Bl.
? Patrinia Scabiosaefolia, L. K.
Dahlia, cultivated.
Vernonia saligna, D. C.
Eupatorium japonicum, Thunb.
Inula cappa, D. C.
Anisopappus chinensis, H. and A.
Artemisia lactifera, Wall.
Senecio japonicus, Thunb.
Senecio Kaempferi, Benth.
Cirsium chinense, Gardn.
Saussurea triangulata, Trantr and Meyer.
Ainsliaea fragrans, Champ.
Clethra canescens, Reimo.
Gelsmium elegans, Benth.
Jacquimontia violacea, Chois.
Solanum Dulcamara, Linn.
Buchnera stricta, Bth.
Torenia Fordii, Hook, f.
Torenia peduncularis, Benth.
Torenia parviflora, Hance.
Vandellia scabra, Benth.
Bonnaya reptans, Sprenge.
Oeginetia nidica, Roxb.
Barleria cristata, Linn.
Chirita obtusa, C. B. C.
Justicea procumbens, Linn.
Clerodendron canescens, Wall.

Plectranthus "eff strictat graciliflora Benth."

Perilla ocimoides, L.

Lophanthus rugosus, F. Mez.

Commelina bengalensis?

Wickstroemia nutans, Champ.

Boehmeria platyphylla, Don.

Carex scaposa Hook f.

Hymenoplyllum javanicum, Spreng.

Polypodium lineare, Thunb.

Vittaris elongata, Sw.

Lycopodium Hamiltonii, Spreng.

The following were collected by Mr. Bourne close to Su-liu and will give an idea of the flora of that spot 800 ft. above the sea. Mr. Ford was kind enough to identify the specimens.

Drymoglossum carnosum Hook.

Pterostigma grandiflorum Benth.

Geophila reniformis D. Don.

Antidesma japonicum Sieb. et Zucc.

Millettia nitida Benth.

Lasianthus Fordii Oliv.

Rhushypoleuca Champ.

Rhodomyrtus tormentosa.

Triumphetta rhomboidea.

Clerodendron lividum.

Paliurus Aubletii.

Psychotria serpens.

Neustanthus Chinensis Benth.

Neustanthus phaseoloides Benth.

Desmodium Gardneri Benth.

and a new and beautiful species of Clematis,
found growing on the temple wall. Mr. Ford
says that this is the same as a specimen
collected by him at Lo-fou in 1883 and
referred to Kew, whence nothing has been
heard regarding it.

Printed by KELLY & WALSH, Limited

www.ingramcontent.com/pod-product-compliance
Lightning Source LLC
Chambersburg PA
CBHW031808090426
42739CB00008B/1219